Some Day

"Healing Hearts" Series

Written by

Janice Jobey

Dedicated to my dear niece, Lora Elizabeth

To children everywhere who have suffered losing a loved one––

May you find peace and healing.

Copyright 2017

Early Learning Innovations, LLC

Bringing Life to Early Childhood

Copyright 2017

Early Learning Innovations, LLC

This book offers a platform to begin the difficult process of helping children say "good-bye" to a dearest loved one(s) whether it is someone who has already died or someone preparing to die. While death is certain to come, it is rarely welcomed. We all want to live long and happy lives with our nearest and dearest. So, letting go and learning to continue to live is not an easy task, even for adults. Children have fewer cognitive resources in grasping this abstract concept. Helping children involves keeping memories alive so the person continues to live "within the heart" long after the loved one is gone.

Written in the "loved one's" voice, this book allows the person who is or has "transitioned to the next life" to speak to the child. The diverse images convey the fact that they are not alone in their experience and children from all around share their feelings. Loved ones and children are supported in making their way through this traumatic event.

Look for more books in the "Healing Hearts" series – divorce, grief and loss, children separated by incarcerated parents, and other topics.

Get Ready to read "Some Day"!

* Don't feel the need to read through the whole book...a page or two at a time can be sufficient considering the deep emotional aspect of this topic. **NOTE:** Written in the "loved one's" voice, this book allows the person who is or has "transitioned to the next life" to speak to the child. Please personalize "loved one" with the name of your "loved one".

* The **Conversational Extenders** at the bottom of each page provide communication support for those assisting children through the trauma experienced by having lost a loved one. These conversational opportunities provide both adult and child words that may be very difficult.

* **GET READY!** Have a notebook and pen and write down the child's responses to the questions on the Conversational Extenders! This will provide a great foundation for making a memory book.

* **The Personal Extenders** at the end of the story, allows the child to make their own pages to add to the book. Use drawings or photos to illustrate. The **Conversational Extenders** and your notes can be a great tool for helping the child with personalizing this book.

* Read the section in the back of the book about **"Talking to Children about Death"**. These are suggestions ONLY, as there are many ways to approach the topic of death and are meant only to support you in this topic. Every family will have their own traditions, strengths, coping mechanisms, and resources that should also be used.

* Discuss the **"pumping heart"** and the **"feeling heart"** and while the same, they are different. The "pumping heart" may actually feel the hurt of the "feeling heart". "Heart" can be spoken of in the physical sense as well as in the emotional sense.

* This book is NOT a substitute for mental health services that may also be beneficial to a child suffering a loss. This book does provide an **opening for discussion** and help the child to realize that talking about the loved one is healthy.

* Be sure to also read our companion book, **"Me Without You"**!

Some day, I'll be gone
And your heart will hurt;
But please remember everyday:
I'll be in your heart always,
And I'll be with you everyday.

Conversational Extenders:

* What does your heart feel like? Draw a picture of your feelings.

* How do you think a loved one can stay with us?

* How will you feel knowing that your loved one can live in your heart?

Some day, you might see a pretty butterfly,
And you might think of me,
And remember the day when two fluttered by.

Conversational Extenders:

* What is a special "moment" you shared with your loved one that no one else has? When that "moment" happened, how did you feel?

Run and gently catch one for me!

Conversational Extenders:

* What can you do to continue to enjoy that "special moment"?

Some day, you might hear our favorite song,
And you might think of me.
And recall how we sang out loud
As we traveled along.

Conversational Extenders:

* Do/Did you and your loved one have a special song or songs that you enjoyed singing? Where did you sing them? How did that make you feel? How does singing/music make you feel?

Go ahead and sing along to our favorite song.

Conversational Extenders:

* What song will you sing to help you remember your loved one?
* Who will sing along with you?

Some day, you might catch
a sweet scent;
And you might think of me.
You'll remember how we cuddled.

Conversational Extenders:

* What scent reminds you of your loved one?

* How did it feel to be cuddled, loved, or hugged by your loved one?

Go ahead and let that scent take you back to all the times we snuggled.

Conversational Extenders:

* Can you close your eyes and remember how those snuggles felt?
* Who else can you snuggle with when you need a hug?

Some day, you might lay your head on my pillow;
And you might think of me.
You'll suddenly remember the way it felt to hold me close.

Conversational Extenders:

* How does it feel to curl up in bed or on a couch/chair or with a pillow that belonged to your loved one? What memories do you have? How did that make you feel to help closely by that person?

Take that pillow and hold it tight and dream of me by your side tonight.

Conversational Extenders:

* How can you go to sleep with happy memories of your loved one?

Some day, you might take a bite of my favorite cookie; And you might think of me. You'll remember all the times we baked and nibbled and giggled.

Conversational Extenders:

* Did you enjoy special foods with your loved one? Which ones? Did you make any of them together? What are your memories? Tell a story about cooking with your loved one or a special food that your loved one enjoyed.

Please eat that cookie and Take a bite for me!

Conversational Extenders:

* What foods can you cook and enjoy that will bring happy memories?

*   Who else will enjoy cooking or baking with you and talking about your loved one?

Some day, you might think you see me at a park;
And you might think of me.
You'll remember how we liked to climb, and swing, and slide.

Conversational Extenders:

*   Have you ever seen someone that reminded you of your loved one? Even if you didn't know them? How does/did that make you feel?

*   What are some memories you have of playing with your loved one?

So take a walk or swing up high! It'll do your heart good! (I promise!)

Conversational Extenders:

*   A quiet walk or swing is good for thinking and processing our thoughts.

*   How is exercise good for your "pumping heart"?

*   How can walking or swinging (or similar activity) be good for our "feeling heart"?

*   What activity would you like to do for your "pumping heart" and your "feeling heart"?

Some day, you might see a pretty flower;
And you might think of me.
You'll remember how we dug in the dirt and planted seeds.

Conversational Extenders:

*   Did you ever work in a garden or similar activity with your loved one? What memories do you have?

*   What flower did your loved one like? What flower reminds you of your loved one?

Please plant more seeds and grow more flowers and always think of me!

Conversational Extenders:

*   Planting flowers can be a way to remember that our loved one can still "live" in our hearts. What would you like to plant to remember your loved one?

Some day, you might pick up our favorite bedtime book;
And you might think of me.
You'll remember how I tucked you in with prayers and kisses.

Conversational Extenders:

*   Did you have a favorite book to read with your loved one? What was it? Do you have a memory about reading a book or playing a game with your loved one?

Go ahead and read our book and say a prayer for me.

Conversational Extenders:

* Who can you read this book with now? Who else is there to tuck you in at night?

* To pray means "to ask". What do you ask for your loved one?

Every day, you'll find me everywhere and in everything; And you'll think of me... and miss me.

And sometimes you'll want to cry because your heart is sad.

Conversational Extenders:

* What do you do when you feel sad? (It's okay to feel sad and to miss our loved ones).

* Who can you talk to when you feel sad? Who else feels sad?

Go ahead, and cry awhile....
But then take a moment to smile and remember that I want you to be happy.

Conversational Extenders:

*   It's okay to smile and be happy even when we might be sad. What can you be happy about? What would your loved one like for you to do that would make you smile? How do you think that would make them feel?

Some day, I'll be gone
And your heart will hurt;
But please remember everyday:
I'll be in your heart always,
And I'll be with you everyday.

Conversational Extenders:

*   What are some ways to know that your loved one is with you? What can you do when you feel sad?

Some day, you might

See/hear/feel/do _____

_____ ;

And you might think of me.
You'll remember how

_____

_____ .

Personal Extenders

* Fill in the blank with something that reminds the child about their loved one and then complete the sentence with a memory of a shared experience associated with that item.

* Draw a picture or paste a photo

Go ahead and

_____

Personal Extenders

* Fill in the blank with how the child can continue to remember that loved one through that shared experience.

* Draw a picture or paste a photo of the child doing that activity or experience.

Some day, you might

See/hear/feel/do _____

_____ ;

And you might think of me.
You'll remember how

_____

_____ .

Personal Extenders

* Fill in the blank with something that reminds the child about their loved one and then complete the sentence with a memory of a shared experience associated with that item.

* Draw a picture or paste a photo

Go ahead and

_____

Personal Extenders

* Fill in the blank with how the child can continue to remember that loved one through that shared experience.

* Draw a picture or paste a photo of the child doing that activity or experience.

Some day, I'll be gone
And your heart will hurt;
But please remember everyday:
I'll be in your heart always,
And I'll be with you everyday.

Personal Extenders

* Discuss with the child how it feels to know that their loved one is always with them.

* Draw a picture or paste a photo of the child with their loved one.

Talking to Children About Death

Young children are often touched by death . . . a grandparent, a parent, a neighbor, a distant relative, a pet . . . someone they know dies. Death is a difficult concept for young children to grasp. They begin to question, develop their own ideas and express their feelings in various ways. Losing a close family member is especially difficult. Understanding how children understand death developmentally, can help adults support young children with the loss of a loved one.

Infants and Toddlers are not able to understand death but may respond to the separation of a close caregiver. Maintaining routines and consistent care giving is very important.

Preschoolers are unable to understand that death is a permanent state, so patience and gentle reminders that the loved one is gone but that memories last forever will help. Because they may not have words to express their feelings, thoughts, or fears, you might see behavior expressed in play, behavior, or they might exhibit emotional reactions or physical symptoms.

School-agers can understand death and can think about this concept. However, their understanding may not be accurate. Death might be personified as a "boogey man", or may believe that they are to blame, or fear that they will be left alone. School-agers will need help with expressing their thoughts and fears and gentle support in correcting misconceptions. Children will pick up on how others are handling the loss and will imitate those responses.

Here are some ideas and suggestions that may help loved ones say goodbye or help surviving loved ones to talk to a child about death.

What is Dead?

1. Simple, honest answers are the best. Answer openly and truthfully. Children need answers in terms they can understand. Try this: "When someone is dead, it means they aren't alive. They can't eat, sleep, move, or feel anything."

2. "Going to sleep", "we lost our dad", and similar explanations can cause confusion and fear in the child. Will he die if he goes to sleep? If Daddy "goes away" on a trip, will he die?"

3. A "dead" state is hard for a young child to comprehend. Never to walk again, never to breathe again is an unchanging state.

Where is _____ now?

1. What happens to a person when they die can be confusing to a child. Again a simple answer such as "The body is put in a box and then into a hole in the ground in the cemetery. His name will be on a tombstone in the grave." But your loved one's memories can "live" on in our hearts.

2. Support the child with the family's personal religious beliefs. While answers like "he's gone to heaven" can be confusing to the child, it can be helpful to use concrete terms as discussed in the previous section.

3. Visiting the cemetery or place of interment is a good idea. This allows the child to understand your answers. It's also a way of remembering the one who has died.

Why do people die?

1. A child may ask this after he has thought about death for awhile. "If my grandma died because she 'got sick', then I might die too if I get sick."
2. You can discuss old age, chronic diseases or catastrophic illness, and accidents with your child. Reassure him that just because a person "gets sick" doesn't mean he'll die.

Other ideas that work

1. Allow your child to pretend play about death. This is a child's way of working out fears and answers to questions.

2. Discuss feelings openly and honestly with your child. Accept and acknowledge his feelings whether negative or positive. Also, talk about how you feel. "I was very sad when grandma died. I miss her a lot. You look sad too." A child may need to talk about this often.

3. Let the child tell a story about the person who has died. Write it down for him.

4. Visit the cemetery, take flowers, and talk openly and honestly about his death.

5. Answer questions simply. If and when he wants more detail, he'll ask more questions.

6. Make a memory book, compiling memories and photos.

Death is a natural occurrence in life just as birth is. Remember to let the child learn in his way . . . by seeing, doing and touching.

Copyright 2017 Early Learning Innovations, LLC

About the Author
Janice S. Jobey, M.S., M.S., CCPS

Janice Jobey is an early childhood expert specializing in literacy, learning, and mental health. Her own childhood experiences with hearing and speech challenges has provided passion in promoting phonological awareness in young children through everyday experiences. Her vast experiences from childhood to "grand-mother-hood" provide the basis for her books and energetic speaking engagements. Janice writes curriculum for infants, toddlers, preschoolers, and parent engagement. Her 35 years of teaching experience spans from infants to adults and working with children with special needs. She holds graduate degrees in child development and education. She lives in rural Oklahoma where she enjoys writing books and curriculum, spending time in her gardens, and playing with her grandchildren.

Contact Janice Jobey, M.S., M.S., CCPS

janjobey@gmail.com

www.earlylearning.today

Copyright 2017 Early Learning Innovations, LLC

Other Titles by Janice Jobey

Me: Learning and Growing
Soft to Touch
My Senses

Family Love
Oh Grana!
Oh Poppa!
Snug as a Bug
Dancing On Daddy's Shoes
Rocking in Mama's Arms

Woodland Wonder
Woodland Riddles
Woodland ABC's
Fox in the City

Pet Set
Pet ABCs
Pet Riddles
Pig Prince
Pet Shop

Spring Set
Flower Garden ABC
Spring Shorts
Spring Senses

Me and You
Rules Keep Us Safe
Just Look at My Face

Pretend Fun
A Princess Needs a Crown

Healing Hearts
These 3 Things
Some Day
Me Without You

Healthy Me
Eat The Rainbow

And many more!

www.ingramcontent.com/pod-product-compliance
Lightning Source LLC
Chambersburg PA
CBHW060759090426
42736CB00002B/94